Role-Play Revision for GCSE Spanish

T. P. Murray

CASSELL

To Harry and Eleanor

First published 1990 by Cassell Publishers Limited
Artillery House, Artillery Row, London SW1P 1RT, England

British Library Cataloguing in Publication Data
Murray, T. P. (Terry P.), *1948–*
  Role-play revision for GCSE Spanish
  1. Spoken Spanish language
  I. Title
  468.3´421

ISBN 0-304-31874-4

Typeset by Litho Link Limited, Welshpool, Powys, Wales.
Printed and bound in Great Britain by Cox & Wyman Ltd,
Reading.

Contents

To the teacher and the pupil

I have selected the role-play situations and prompts in this book using my experience as a teacher of GCSE languages in a comprehensive school and as a Chief Examiner with a GCSE board. The material in this book covers the syllabuses of all the UK exam groups.

The role-play part of the oral test requires a lot of practice and it is not always easy to find prompts in English to practise on. It is for this reason that this book has been written. Each unit has been divided into three parts:

- Essential vocabulary.
- A list of English prompts.
- A list of suggested answers to those prompts
  (at the back of the book).

Needless to say, there is always more than one way of communicating an idea in a foreign language. I have selected the expression that I feel GCSE/Standard candidates will find easiest to remember and to use.

I suggest that the pupil approach each unit as follows. First, learn the vocabulary section. You will find that you will be floundering later on if you don't. Then, look at the English prompts. Don't try to work through a whole section. Take, say, five or ten prompts. See if you can answer them and then look up the answers at the back of the book to see how you fared. The book can be used for pair-work in class and is ideal for homework setting.

In your exam, you may have to express a feeling as well as communicate a fact. For instance, the prompt might say:

'Say that you do not agree and ask to see the manager.'

To cater for this, I have included a special section called 'Expressing your feelings'. In addition, there is a list of useful phrases, which will be valuable in many role-play situations.

¡Suerte!

Terry Murray
Head of Modern Languages, Edgecliff School, Staffordshire
Joint Chief Examiner in Spanish for MEG

Useful phrases

¿Dónde está . . .?	Where is . . .?
¿Cómo se va a . . .?	How do I get to . . .?
¿A qué hora es . . .?	What time is . . .?
¿A qué distancia está . . .?	How far is . . .?
¿Cuánto tiempo . . .?	How long . . .?
¿Puede Vd . . .?	Can you . . .?
¿Puede Vd. decirme . . .?	Can you tell me . . .?
¿Quiere Vd . . .?	Please will you . . .?
¿Quiere Vd. darme . . .?	Please will you give me . . .?
Me gustaría . . .	I would like . . .
Estoy buscando . . .	I am looking for . . .
¿Puede Vd. ayudarme?	Can you help me?
¿Quiere Vd. repetirlo?	Would you repeat that, please?
¿Quiere Vd. hablar más despacio?	Please speak more slowly.
Entiendo.	I understand.
No entiendo.	I don't understand.
¡Vale!	OK!
¿Hay . . .?	Is there . . .?
He perdido . . .	I have lost . . .
Hay que . . .	It is necessary to . . .

Expressing your feelings

¡Cuidado!	Be careful!
¡Qué lástima!	What a pity!
Prefiero . . .	I prefer . . .
No me gusta . . .	I don't like . . .
Detesto . . .	I hate . . .
Me gusta . . .	I like . . .
Me encanta . . .	I love . . .
Espero que . . .	I hope that . . .
Me gustó.	I liked it.
No me gustó.	I didn't like it.
Me decepcionó.	It was disappointing.
Estoy contento(a).	I am happy.
Me he olvidado . . .	I have forgotten . . .
¡Perdón!	I am sorry!
Lo siento pero . . .	I am sorry but . . .
¡Socorro!	Help!
¡De acuerdo!	Agreed!
Estoy de acuerdo.	I agree.
No estoy de acuerdo.	I don't agree.
¡Enhorabuena!	Congratulations!
¡Salud!	Good health!
¡Suerte!	Good luck!
¡Buen viaje!	Have a good trip!
¡Que aproveche!	Enjoy your meal!
Lo siento mucho.	I am very sorry.
¡Qué sorpresa!	What a surprise!
¡De nada!	Don't mention it!

Estoy harto(a).	I am fed up.
¡No se preocupe! ¡No te preocupes!	Don't worry!
¡Que se divierta! ¡Que te diviertas!	Have a good time!
¡Menos mal!	It's just as well!
¡Buena idea!	Good idea!
Acepto su (tu) oferta.	I accept your offer.
No acepto su (tu) oferta.	I refuse your offer.
Creo que sí.	I think so.
No lo creo.	I don't think so.
Me da igual.	I don't mind.
Me aburro.	I am bored.
Tengo miedo.	I am frightened.
Estoy enfadado(a).	I am angry.

Public transport

VOCABULARIO ESENCIAL

BUYING TICKETS

first-class ticket	el billete de primera clase
second-class ticket	el billete de segunda clase
single ticket	el billete de ida
return ticket	el billete de ida y vuelta
ticket-office	el despacho de billetes

FACILITIES

buffet	la cafetería
information office	la oficina de información
left-luggage office	la consigna
lost property office	la oficina de objetos perdidos
timetable	el horario
waiting-room	la sala de espera

TRAVELLING BY RAIL

carriage	el vagón
compartment	el departamento
dining-car	el coche-comedor
platform	el andén
porter	el mozo
railway	el ferrocarril
sleeping-car	el coche-cama

TRAVELLING BY AIR

air hostess	la azafata
airport	el aeropuerto
flight	el vuelo

TRAVELLING BY BUS, UNDERGROUND OR TAXI

bus	el autocar / el autobús
bus station	la estación de autobuses
bus stop	la parada de autobuses
taxi rank	la parada de taxis
underground	el metro
underground station	la estación del metro

TRAVELLING BY SEA

hovercraft	el aerodeslizador
ferry	el ferry
ship	el barco

VERBS

to arrive	llegar
to book	reservar
to change (i.e. trains)	hacer transbordo
to fly	volar
it is necessary	hay que
to leave	salir
to leave (e.g. luggage)	dejar
to miss (i.e. a train)	perder
to stop	parar
to wait	esperar

OTHER	WORDS		
bag	el bolso	Have a good trip!	¡Buen viaje!
by air	en avión	late	tarde
by train	en tren	luggage	el equipaje (m)
direct	directo	passport	el pasaporte
early	temprano	seat	el asiento
entrance	la entrada	suitcase	la maleta
exit	la salida	taken (i.e. a seat)	ocupado
free	libre	traveller	el viajero

Te toca a ti

1 Ask for a second-class single to Madrid.

2 Ask for a first-class return to Valencia.

3 Say you want two tickets.

4 Find out if there is a bus/train to Barcelona.

5 Find out what time it arrives/leaves.

6 Find out the times of the trains to Madrid.

7 Say you would like to reserve a ticket.

8 Say that you have a reserved ticket.

9 Find out where the station/the bus station/the underground station is.

10 Ask how long the journey takes.

11 Find out when the next flight is.

12 Ask where the ticket office is.

13 Ask where the information office is.

14 Find out where the left luggage/lost property office is.

15 Ask where the Madrid train leaves from.

16 Find out which platform the Valencia train leaves from.

17 Ask where the taxi rank/bus stop is.

18 Find out if there is a seat free in the carriage.

19 Say that the seat is taken.

20 Find out what time the plane leaves/arrives.

21 Say that you would like to take a taxi.

22 Ask where you can find a taxi.

23 Find out if the train is direct.

24 Ask if it is necessary to change.

25 Ask where you must change.

26 Say you want a cheap hotel.

27 Ask for the buffet.

28 Find out when the next/first/last bus leaves.

29 Say you want a non-smoking compartment.

30 Ask where you can put your luggage.

31 Ask if this is the right platform for the Santander train.

32 Ask where you should get off.

33 Find out if there is a dining-car/a sleeping-car.

34 Ask if there is a reduction/a supplement.

35 Find out where the toilets are.

36 Find out where the waiting-room is.

37 Ask if you can leave your luggage here.

38 Find out if the flight is late.

39 Ask if the train arrived early.

40 Say that you have lost your ticket.

41 Ask for a map of the underground.

42 Say you will arrive at 10 p.m.

43 Say you will set off at 2 a.m.

44 Ask your friend if he/she has anything to declare.

45 Say that you have just arrived.

46 Say that you will catch the ten o'clock bus.

47 Tell your friend that you tried to phone from the station.

48 Tell your friend that you will phone from the airport.

49 Find out where you can find a porter.

50 Ask the porter to help you with your luggage.

Dos billetes de ida, por favor.

51 Say that you have missed the bus.

52 Find out if the bus goes to the city centre.

Las contestaciones están en la página 63

At the garage / filling station

VOCABULARIO ESENCIAL

BREAKDOWN

battery	**la batería**
brakes	**los frenos**
breakdown	**la avería**
flat (tyre)	**pinchado**
headlight	**el faro**
mechanic	**el mecánico**
puncture	**el pinchazo**
windscreen	**el parabrisas**

ROUTINE STOP

oil	**el aceite**
petrol	**la gasolina**
petrol (four-star)	**súper**
petrol (lead-free)	**sin plomo**
pressure (of tyres)	**la presión**
road-map	**el mapa de carreteras**
toilets	**los servicios**

tyre	**el neumático**
water	**agua** (f)

ROADS

A-road	**la carretera nacional**
motorway	**la autopista**

VERBS

to break down	**averiarse**
to check (i.e. the oil)	**comprobar**
to clean	**limpiar**
to fill (e.g. the petrol tank)	**llenar**
to park	**aparcar, estacionar**
to repair	**reparar**
to run out of (e.g. petrol)	**quedarse sin**
to work (i.e. the brakes)	**funcionar**

Te toca a ti

1 Ask for 20 litres of high-grade petrol.

2 Ask for 10 litres of lead-free petrol.

3 Ask the attendant to fill up the tank.

4 Ask the attendant to check the oil.

5 Ask the attendant to check the tyres.

6 Ask the attendant to check the water.

7 Find out where the toilets are.

8 Ask if they sell road-maps.

9 Find out if you are on the right road for Madrid.

10 Ask which way to go for Málaga.

11 Find out if the road is an A-road or a motorway.

12 Find out where you can park.

13 Say your car has broken down.

14 Say you have left it two kilometres away.

15 Ask if he can help.

16 Ask if he can fix your car.

17 Ask if there is a mechanic available.

18 Say the brakes don't work.

19 Say you have a puncture.

20 Tell the attendant that a headlight is not working.

21 Say that the windscreen is broken.

22 Say you need a new battery.

23 Find out how much you owe.

24 Ask if you can phone from here.

25 Find out how far Madrid is.

26 Find out where the nearest hotel is.

27 Ask if they sell sweets.

28 Ask the attendant to clean the windscreen.

29 Say you have run out of petrol.

30 Say you have had an accident.

31 Ask how long you will have to wait.

32 Ask how much it will cost.

Las contestaciones están en la página 65

¿Quiere Vd. comprobar el agua?

At the customs

VOCABULARIO ESENCIAL

LUGGAGE		present	el regalo
bag	el bolso	watch	el reloj
luggage	el equipaje		
suitcase	la maleta	**OTHER WORDS**	
		customs	la aduana
PROPERTY		customs officer	el aduanero
passport	el pasaporte	to declare	declarar
perfume	el perfume		

Te toca a ti

1 Say you are English/Irish/Scottish/Welsh.

2 Say you have nothing to declare.

3 Say you would like to declare a camera.

4 Tell the officer that you have two suitcases and a bag.

5 Say that the suitcase is yours.

6 Tell the officer that there are clothes and presents in your suitcase.

7 Say that you bought the watch in Switzerland two weeks ago.

8 Tell the officer that the perfume cost four thousand pesetas.

9 Ask if he/she wants to see your passport.

10 Tell the officer that you will be in Spain for two weeks.

11 Say that you are here on holiday.

Las contestaciones están en la página 67

At the campsite

EQUIPMENT

battery	**la pila**
butane gas	**el gas butano**
caravan	**la caravana**
corkscrew	**el sacacorchos**
tent	**la tienda**
tin-opener	**el abrelatas**

FACILITIES

drinking water	**el agua potable** (f)
dustbin	**el cubo de basura**
electric socket	**la toma de corriente**
facility	**la instalación**
space (i.e. for tent)	**el sitio**
toilets	**los servicios**
washing-machine	**la lavadora**

OTHER WORDS

campsite	**el camping**

clean	**limpio**
dirty	**sucio**
extra payment	**el suplemento**
match (for lighting a fire)	**la cerilla**
owner (of site)	**el dueño**
rules	**el reglamento**
shade	**la sombra**
well-lit	**bien iluminado**

VERBS

to camp	**acampar**
to do the washing-up	**lavar los platos**
to go camping	**hacer camping**
to need	**necesitar**
to put up (a tent)	**armar / montar (una tienda)**
to stay	**quedarse**

Te toca a ti

1 Say you would like to reserve a pitch.

2 Ask if you can camp here.

3 Find out if they have space for a tent.

4 Say you have a tent/caravan.

5 Ask how much it is for a tent, two adults, four children and a car.

6 Say you would like to stay for two days.

7 Say you are alone.

8 Say that you will arrive the day after tomorrow.

9 Tell the warden that you will leave on Saturday.

10 Ask where you can put your tent.

11 Say you would like a pitch in the shade.

12 Say you are English/Irish/Scottish/Welsh.

13 Ask if he/she wants to see your passport.

14 Find out when you must pay.

15 Say you would like to pay now.

16 Ask how you get to the campsite.

17 Find out if there are hot showers.

¿Vd. ha perdido la llave de su caravana? ¿Le presto un abrelatas?

18 Say you want a pitch near the toilets.

19 Find out where you can find drinking water.

20 Ask where you can wash clothes/dishes.

21 Ask about the regulations.

22 Say that your pitch is too near the dustbins.

23 Ask if you can borrow a tin-opener/corkscrew/some matches.

24 Ask if you can put up your tent over there.

25 Find out where the nearest electric socket is.

26 Ask how much it is per person.

27 Say it is too expensive.

28 Ask if there is a washing-machine on the site.

29 Ask if they serve hot meals.

30 Find out if there is a shop on the site.

31 Ask if you can light a fire.

32 Tell the warden that you are very pleased with the campsite.

33 Ask if the campsite has lots of facilities.

34 Say you need butane gas.

35 Say you need batteries.

36 Find out if the campsite is well-lit at night.

37 Ask if the campsite is closed at night.

38 Ask if you have to pay extra for that.

Las contestaciones están en la página 67

At the youth hostel

VOCABULARIO ESENCIAL

BEDDING
blanket	la manta
sheet	la sábana
sleeping-bag	el saco de dormir

PLACES
bathroom	el cuarto de baño
dining-room	el comedor
dormitory	el dormitorio
kitchen	la cocina
shower	la ducha
toilets	los servicos

AT RECEPTION
all year	todo el año
bed	la cama
closed	cerrado
form (to fill in)	la ficha
full	lleno
open	abierto
per day	por día
per night	por noche

per person	por persona
regulations	el reglamento

OTHER WORDS
breakfast	el desayuno
complaint	la queja
dustbin	el cubo de basura
hot water	agua caliente (f)
meal	la comida
valuables	los objetos de valor
youth hostel	el albergue juvenil

VERBS
to book	reservar
to cook	cocinar
to fill in (e.g. a form)	rellenar
to have one's evening meal	cenar
to hire	alquilar
to leave (depart)	marcharse
to pay	pagar
to sleep	dormir

Te toca a ti

1 Say you have booked a bed.

2 Say you have not reserved a bed.

3 Ask if there are any free beds.

4 Say you will leave tomorrow (the day after tomorrow).

5 Say you will stay for three nights.

6 Tell the warden that there are two boys and two girls in your party.

7 Say you are English/Irish/Scottish/Welsh.

8 Find out how much it is per person.

9 Ask if there are shops nearby.

10 Find out if there are showers/a kitchen in the hostel.

11 Ask where the toilets/the dust-bins are.

12 Tell the warden that you would like to pay now/later/tomorrow/on leaving.

13 Find out what time breakfast/lunch/dinner is served.

14 Ask what time the hostel closes.

¿Puedo alquilar una sábana también, por favor?

15 Ask what time the office opens in the morning.

16 Ask what the regulations are.

17 Tell the warden that you have a sleeping-bag.

18 Say that you would like to hire a sleeping-bag/some sheets/ some blankets.

19 Ask where the girls'/boys' dormitory is.

20 Find out if alcohol is allowed.

21 Ask what time you must leave the hostel.

22 Find out if you have to fill in a form.

23 Enquire if there is hot water.

24 Ask what you must do before leaving.

25 Find out where you can leave valuables.

26 Say you have a complaint.

27 Ask the warden if he/she wants to see your card.

28 Find out if the hostel is full.

29 Ask if the hostel is open all year.

30 Enquire if you can cook in the hostel.

31 Ask if they serve meals.

32 Ask directions to the dining-room.

33 Ask where you can leave your bicycle.

34 Say you are sorry. You do not want a bed upstairs. Ask for a bed on the ground floor.

Las contestaciones están en la página 69

At the doctor's/at the scene of an accident

VOCABULARIO ESENCIAL

BUYING MEDICINE

antiseptic	**el antiséptico**
aspirin	**la aspirina**
bandage	**la venda**
chemist's	**la farmacia**
cotton wool	**el algodón hidrófilo**
cream (i.e. for sores)	**la pomada**
medicine	**la medicina**
plaster (for cuts)	**el esparadrapo**
prescription	**la receta**
receipt	**el recibo**
tablet	**la pastilla**

COMPLAINTS

flu	**la gripe**
to have a cold	**estar constipado(a)**
injured	**herido(a)**
sunburn	**la quemadura del sol**
sunstroke	**la insolación**
temperature	**la fiebre**

SCENE OF AN ACCIDENT

ambulance	**la ambulancia**
collision	**la colisión**
doctor	**el médico**
driving licence	**el permiso de conducir**
fault	**la culpa**

fire	**el incendio**
firemen	**los bomberos**
insurance	**el seguro**
serious	**grave**

OTHER WORDS

better	**mejor**
dentist	**el dentista**
stomach	**el estómago**
throat	**la garganta**
tooth	**el diente/la muela**

VERBS

to be seasick	**estar mareado(a)**
to brake	**frenar**
to break	**romper**
to burn	**quemar**
to cough	**toser**
to cross (e.g. street)	**cruzar**
to cut oneself	**cortarse**
to fall	**caer**
to feel	**sentirse**
to hurt oneself	**hacerse daño**
to knock over	**atropellar**
to stay in bed	**guardar cama**
to sting	**picar**
to vomit	**vomitar**

Te toca a ti

1 Ask if he/she can help you.

2 Ask him/her to phone a doctor.

3 Ask him/her to phone for an ambulance.

4 Say you need to see a dentist.

5 Say you would like to see the doctor.

6 Say you have had an accident.

7 Say you have toothache.

8 Say you have a sore throat.

9 Say you have a headache.

10 Say you have a pain in your stomach.

11 Say you have broken your arm/leg.

12 Say he has broken his arm/leg.

13 Say you have a cold.

14 Say you have burnt yourself.

15 Say you have burnt your arm.

16 Say he has sunstroke/sunburn.

17 Say she has flu.

18 Say you have cut yourself.

19 Say you have cut your leg.

20 Say that you fell.

21 Say that you had a car accident.

22 Say that you have a temperature.

23 Say that you are seasick.

24 Say that you have been stung.

25 Say that you have a cough.

26 Say that you have been sick three times.

27 Say that your friend is injured.

28 Ask if you must come back to see the doctor again.

29 Find out if you have to stay in bed.

30 Find out if you need a prescription.

31 Find out where the chemist's is.

32 Ask for a receipt.

33 Find out how long you must take the tablets for.

34 Say you would like to buy some cotton wool, a bandage, some plasters and some antiseptic.

35 Say that your sister feels ill.

36 Ask for some aspirin.

37 When asked how long you have been ill, say for two hours/ since yesterday.

38 Ask how often you should take the tablets.

39 Say that you feel ill/better.

40 Find out if he has anything for a sore throat.

41 Say that you are taking no medicines.

42 Say that you have insurance.

43 Ask him/her to phone the police/fire brigade.

44 Say that the accident was serious.

45 Say it was not your fault; say it was the fault of the other driver.

46 Find out if they sell a cream for sunburn.

47 Say that your father braked but there was a collision.

48 Say there was a fire in the engine.

49 Say that your father's driving licence is at the hotel.

50 Say that a cyclist knocked over an old man who was crossing the street.

51 Say that it hurts.

Las contestaciones están en la página 71

¿Quiere Vd. llamar una ambulancia?

Shopping for food and drink

SHOPS

baker's	la panadería
butcher's	la carnicería
chemist's	la farmacia
department store	los almacenes
fishmonger's	la pescadería
food store	la tienda de comestibles
market	el mercado
supermarket	el supermercado
tobacconist's	el estanco

FRUIT

apple	la manzana
apricot	el albaricoque
banana	el plátano
cherry	la ciruela
fruit	la fruta
grape	la uva
melon	el melón
orange	la naranja
peach	el melocotón
pear	la pera
pineapple	la piña
strawberry	la fresa

VEGETABLES

carrot	la zanahoria
cauliflower	la coliflor
green beans	las judías verdes
lettuce	la lechuga
mushroom	el champiñon
onion	la cebolla
peas	los guisantes
potato	la patata
vegetable	la legumbre

MEAT

beef	la carne de vaca
chicken	el pollo
garlic sausage	el chorizo
ham	el jamón
lamb	el cordero
meat	la carne
rabbit	el conejo
steak	el bistec

DESSERT		OTHER WORDS	
cake	el pastel	butter	la mantequilla
cheese	el queso	egg	el huevo
dessert	el postre	loaf	la barra
ice-cream	el helado	pepper	la pimienta
		salt	la sal
DRINK		seafood	los mariscos
beer	la cerveza	sugar	el azúcar
coffee	el café		
drink	la bebida	VERBS	
fruit juice	el zumo de fruta	to choose	escoger
milk	la leche	to give back	devolver
mineral water	agua mineral (f)	to pay	pagar
tea	el té	to take (i.e. to buy)	llevarse
wine	el vino		

Te toca a ti

1 Say you would like a loaf of bread.

2 Ask how much it is.

3 Say you would like to buy some cakes.

4 Ask for five hundred grammes of ham.

5 Say you would like some beef.

6 Ask for two hundred and fifty grammes of garlic sausage.

7 Find out if there is a grocer's shop open in the area.

8 Say you would like to buy some cigarettes for your father.

9 Ask for two hundred grammes of cherries/bananas/oranges/peaches/pears/apples/strawberries/apricots/grapes.

10 Ask for a pineapple/a melon.

11 Find out where you can buy vegetables.

12 Ask for a pound of green beans/onions/peas/ potatoes/mushrooms/carrots/a cauliflower.

13 Ask for a lettuce.

14 Find out if there is a butcher's shop nearby.

15 Ask for a chicken/rabbit/five hundred grammes of steak.

16 Ask if the meat is good in that shop.

17 Find out where you can buy seafood.

18 Find out if they have French wine.

19 Buy two litres of red wine and one litre of white wine.

20 Ask for five litres of beer.

21 Ask for coffee.

22 Ask for a bottle of mineral water.

23 Say you would like some fruit juice.

24 Ask for a litre of milk.

25 Ask for a packet of tea.

26 Ask for a dozen eggs.

27 Find out where you can buy salt/pepper.

28 Ask for two hundred grammes of cheese.

Compré este queso aquí. ¡No es bueno!

29 Say you are buying food for a picnic.

30 Ask for two hundred grammes of butter.

31 Find out if they sell sweets/chocolate.

32 Ask for a packet of sugar.

33 Say you do not like it and that you are not going to buy it.

34 Say it is too dear.

35 Say he/she has given you too much/very little.

36 Say you will take it.

37 Say you want nothing else.

38 Find out how much you owe.

39 Ask for change for the telephone.

40 Say you bought this cheese here. Say it is not nice. Ask for your money back.

41 Say you only have a thousand-peseta note.

42 Ask if you can choose the fruit that you want.

43 Say a little bigger, please.

44 Ask if he/she has anything cheaper.

45 Find out where the cash desk is.

46 Ask for a box/plastic bag.

47 Find out if you can pay with a cheque or credit card.

48 Ask if they are open on Sunday.

49 Find out what time they open/close.

Las contestaciones están en la página 73

Shopping for clothes and toiletries

MATERIALS

cotton	**el algodón**
leather	**el cuero**
nylon	**el nilón**
wool	**la lana**

SIZE OF CLOTHES

big	**grande**
long	**largo**
short	**corto**
size	**la talla**
size (of shoes)	**el número**
small	**pequeño**
tight	**estrecho**
too	**demasiado**
wide	**ancho**

BAD-WEATHER CLOTHES

anorak	**el anorak**
coat	**el abrigo**
glove	**el guante**
hat	**el sombrero**
jumper	**el jersey**
raincoat	**el impermeable**
scarf	**la bufanda**

GOOD-WEATHER CLOTHES

shorts	**el pantalón corto**

swimming-costume	**el traje de baño**
T-shirt	**la camiseta**

ON YOUR FEET

boot	**la bota**
shoe	**el zapato**
slipper	**la zapatilla**
sock	**el calcetín**

OTHER CLOTHES

blouse	**la blusa**
dress	**el vestido**
dressing-gown	**la bata (woman's), el batín (man's)**
jacket	**la chaqueta**
jeans	**los vaqueros**
pyjamas	**el pijama**
shirt	**la camisa**
skirt	**la falda**
suit	**el traje**
tie	**la corbata**
trousers	**los pantalones**

TOILETRIES

comb	**el peine**
shampoo	**el champú**
soap	**el jabón**
toothbrush	**el cepillo de dientes**
toothpaste	**la pasta de dientes**

OTHER WORDS		VERBS	
changing cubicle	**el probador**	to make a mistake	**equivocarse**
cheap	**barato**	to put on	**ponerse**
clothes	**la ropa**	to try on	**probarse**
department (of store)	**la sección**	to window-shop	**ir de escaparates**
handkerchief	**el pañuelo**	to wrap up	**envolver**
pair	**el par**		

Te toca a ti

1 Ask what size it is.

2 Ask what size the shoes are.

3 Ask if the shirt is cotton/nylon.

4 Ask if the jersey is made of wool.

5 Say you would like to buy some slippers.

6 Find out if the gloves are made of leather.

7 Say that you like this jacket.

8 Find out where the changing rooms are.

9 Say you would like to try on this pair of trousers.

10 Find out if they have the same skirt in blue.

11 Say the dress is too long/short/tight/wide/big/small.

12 Ask the assistant to gift-wrap the scarf.

13 Find out on which floor the men's department is.

14 Ask for the cash desk.

15 Find out where the lift/exit is.

16 Find out what time they open/close.

17 Ask if you can listen to this record.

18 Request a plastic bag.

19 Ask if you can exchange the coat.

20 Say that it is not your size.

21 Find out if there is another shop nearby.

22 Tell him/her that he/she has made a mistake.

23 Ask you friend which he/she is going to buy.

24 Ask if this T-shirt suits you.

25 Find out where you can buy soap/shampoo/a comb/a toothbrush/toothpaste.

26 Say you would like to window-shop.

27 Say it is too expensive.

28 Say it is very cheap.

29 Ask for your size.

30 Find out if they have anything cheaper.

31 Find out where you should pay.

Las contestaciones están en la página 75

At the cleaner's/ launderette

VOCABULARIO ESENCIAL			
change (for washing-machine)	el cambio	to clean	limpiar
		to dry-clean	impiar en seco
cleaner's	la lavandería, la tintorería	to mend (clothes)	reparar (ropa)
		washing-machine	la lavadora
coin	la moneda	washing-powder	el jabón en polvo
launderette	la lavandería automática		

Te toca a ti

1 Ask if your trousers can be cleaned/dry-cleaned.

2 Ask if your blouse can be mended.

3 Find out how long it will take.

4 Say you would like to wash these clothes.

5 Ask for change for the washing-machine.

6 Find out which coins are needed for the washing-machine.

7 Ask where you can buy washing-powder.

Las contestaciones están en la página 77

At the café/restaurant

ON THE TABLE

cup	la taza
fork	el tenedor
glass	el vaso
knife	el cuchillo
mustard	la mostaza
pepper	la pimienta
plate	el plato
salt	la sal
saucer	el platillo
spoon	la cuchara
tablecloth	el mantel
vinegar	el vinagre

FACILITIES

area outside a café	la terraza
in the shade	en la sombra
in the sun	en el sol
telephone	el teléfono
toilets	los servicios

ORDERING

dessert	el postre
first course	el primer plato
menu	el menú
today's menu	el menú del día
waiter	el camarero

STEAKS

medium	medio hecho
rare	poco hecho
well-done	bien hecho

FOOD

breakfast	el desayuno
chips	las patatas
cucumber	el pepino
ice-cream (vanilla, strawberry, chocolate)	el helado (de vainilla, de fresa, de chocolate)
mussels	las mejillones
oysters	las ostras
pork chop	la chuleta de cerdo
rice	el arroz
salad	la ensalada
sandwich (cheese, ham, garlic sausage)	el bocadillo (de queso, de jamón, de chorizo)
sardine	la sardina
soup	la sopa
trout	la trucha

See also pages 24-5 in the 'Shopping for food' section.

PAYING THE BILL

bill	la cuenta
included	incluido
mistake	el error
owner	el dueño
service	el servicio
tip	la propina

OTHER WORDS		VERBS	
ashtray	el cenicero	to be hungry	tener hambre
Cheers!	¡Salud!	to be thirsty	tener sed
choice	la selección	to book	reservar
delicious	delicioso	to choose	escoger
Enjoy your meal!	¡Que aproveche!	to clean	limpiar
ill	enfermo	to order	pedir
portion	la ración	to smell	oler
tray	la bandeja		

Te toca a ti

1 Call the waiter/waitress and ask for the menu.

2 Say you would like to leave a tip.

3 Say you would like to reserve a table.

4 Say you have reserved a table.

5 Ask the waiter for a cup/saucer/knife/fork/spoon/glass.

6 Say that the tablecloth is dirty.

7 Tell the waiter that you would like to order.

8 Ask the waiter to remove the tray.

9 Ask for the bill.

10 Say 'Cheers!' and 'Enjoy your meal'.

11 Ask the waiter to choose a wine.

12 Find out where the telephone is/the toilets are.

13 Find out if service is included.

14 Say that you are hungry/thirsty.

15 Say that you want your steak rare/medium/well-done.

16 Say that the meal is delicious.

17 Ask what he/she would like for dessert.

18 Say that you feel ill.

19 Ask for the tourist menu.

20 Ask for the menu of the day.

21 Ask for pork chop with onions, peas and chips.

22 Find out if they serve breakfast.

23 Say you would like black/white coffee.

24 Order soup, rabbit, rice/potatoes.

25 Say you would like a cheese/garlic sausage/ham sandwich.

26 Order oysters/mussels.

27 Order trout/sardines.

¿A qué hora se sirve el desayuno, por favor?

28 Say you would like some cucumber in the salad.

29 Ask for cherries/a banana/a melon/an orange/a peach/a pear/an apple/some strawberries/some apricots/some pineapple/some grapes.

30 Order chicken, green beans, mushrooms and carrots.

31 Say you do not like garlic.

32 Tell the waiter that the cauliflower is not nice.

33 Find out if you can have lamb.

34 Find out what drinks they serve.

35 Ask for a litre of white/red wine.

36 Order a half litre of beer.

37 Say you would like some fruit juice/mineral water/milk/tea.

38 Say you would like a boiled/fried/poached/scrambled egg.

39 Ask for salt/pepper/vinegar/mustard.

40 Ask for a portion of ham.

41 Ask the waiter to clean the table.

42 Say you would like to be outside in the sun/shade.

43 Ask for a table for two near the window.

44 Tell the waiter that he has made a mistake.

45 Say you do not understand the menu. Ask what this dish is.

46 Ask him/her to close/open the window.

47 Ask for more.

48 Ask for an ashtray.

49 Tell the waiter he has forgotten the vanilla ice-cream.

50 Ask for change for the telephone.

51 Say the food is cold.

52 Say that your fork is dirty.

53 Say that you want something cool/hot to drink.

54 Say that you are too hot/cold.

55 Say that you only had a lemonade and an orange juice.

56 Ask him to check the bill.

57 Say you are in a hurry. Find out how long it will take.

58 Say that there are four of you.

59 Explain to your friend that this dish is not meat, but fish.

60 Find out if they accept credit cards.

61 Say you did not order any wine.

62 Find out if there is a choice of vegetables.

63 Say that it smells good.

64 Ask your friend if he/she has decided.

65 Say that it is too expensive.

66 Find out which wine he/she would like.

Las contestaciones están en la página 77

At the post office

VOCABULARIO ESENCIAL

ITEMS TO SEND

letter	la carta
packet/parcel	el paquete
postal order	el giro postal
postcard	la postal
telegram	el telegrama

FACILITIES

counter	la ventanilla
phone booth	la cabina telefónica
post-box	el buzón
poste restante	la lista de correos

SENDING THINGS OFF

abroad	al extranjero
address	la dirección, las señas

by air	por avión
forty-peseta stamp	el sello de cuarenta pesetas
United Kingdom	el Reino Unido

OTHER WORDS

coin	la moneda
collection (of mail)	la recogida
fragile	frágil

VERBS

to fill in a form	rellenar una ficha
to post	echar (al correo)
to send	mandar

Te toca a ti

1 Ask where the post office is.

2 Ask if there is a post-box in the post office.

3 Find out how much it costs to send a letter/postcard to England.

4 Say you would like to send a letter to Great Britain.

5 Say you would like to send a parcel.

6 Find out if a packet has arrived for you.

7 Say you would like two forty-peseta stamps.

8 Find out what time they open/close.

9 Ask if there is a letter for you at the poste restante counter.

10 Find out if there is a phone booth here.

11 Say you need coins for a phone call to the United Kingdom.

12 Say that you want to send a telegram.

13 Ask how much it is to send a telegram.

14 Find out how long it takes for a letter to reach the United Kingdom.

15 Ask if there is a special post-box for letters going abroad.

16 Find out where there is a post-box.

17 Say you would like to phone England.

18 Say you would like to buy a postal order.

¿Vd. quiere un millón de pesetas? Hay que rellenar una ficha.

19 Find out which counter you need.

20 Say you want to send the letter by airmail.

21 Find out if you have to fill in a form.

22 Ask if the post office is open on Saturday.

23 Find out if there is a faster service.

24 Ask when the next collection is.

Las contestaciones están en la página 80

On the telephone

VOCABULARIO ESENCIAL			
dialling tone	**el tono de marcar**	phone number	**el número de teléfono**
directory	**la guía telefónica**		
Hello (answering phone)	**¡Dígame!**	reverse-charge call	**la llamada a cobro revertido**
message	**el recado**	to dial	**marcar**
operator	**la operadora**	to hang up	**colgar**
phone call	**la llamada telefónica**	to make a mistake	**equivocarse**

Te toca a ti

1 Find out where the nearest telephone is.

2 Ask for the telephone directory.

3 Ask if you can speak to Juan.

4 Say you can't hear the dialling tone.

5 Ask for the number of the tourist office.

6 Say you would like to speak to the operator.

7 Say you want to make a reverse-charge call.

8 When you have picked up the phone, say hello and say it is Melanie speaking.

9 Ask the caller if he/she wants to leave a message.

10 Say you don't understand. Ask the caller to speak more slowly.

11 Ask the person not to hang up.

12 Say you have got the wrong number.

Las contestaciones están en la página 81

¿Es la operadora? Quiero llamar a Marte, por favor.

At the bank/ exchange office

VOCABULARIO ESENCIAL

MONEY

currency	**la moneda**
pound sterling	**la libra esterlina**
thousand-peseta note	**el billete de mil pesetas**

ITEMS TO TAKE

banker's card	**la tarjeta bancaria**
credit card	**la tarjeta de crédito**
passport	**el pasaporte**
traveller's cheque	**el cheque de viaje**

OTHER WORDS

cashier's desk	**la ventanilla de pagos**

commission	**la comisión**
counter	**la ventanilla**
per cent	**por ciento**
rate of exchange	**el cambio**

VERBS

to be worth	**valer**
to change	**cambiar**
to queue	**hacer cola**
to sign	**firmar**

Te toca a ti

1 Find out where you must queue.

2 Say you want to change some pounds into pesetas.

3 Say you want to change some traveller's cheques into pesetas.

4 Find out at which counter.

5 Ask if it is your turn.

6 Ask what the rate of exchange is.

7 Ask if he/she wants to see your passport.

8 Say you have forgotten your passport.

9 Say you will go and get your passport.

10 Find out where you have to sign.

11 Find out how much the pound is worth.

12 Ask if you must go to the cashier's desk.

13 Say you have a credit card.

14 Say you have a banker's card.

15 Find out if you have to pay a commission.

16 Ask if the commission is ten per cent.

17 Say you would like five-thousand peseta notes.

18 Say you would like some hundred-peseta coins.

19 Tell the clerk that all your money has been stolen.

20 Ask him/her to phone your bank in England.

Las contestaciones están en la página 82

At the police station/ lost property office

VOCABULARIO ESENCIAL

PROPERTY

camera	la máquina fotográfica
handbag	el bolso de mano
passport	el pasaporte
purse	el monedero
ring	el anillo
suitcase	la maleta
wallet	la cartera
watch	el reloj

OTHER WORDS

colour	el color
description	la descripción
form (to fill in)	la ficha
gold	el oro

lost property office	la oficina de objetos perdidos
make (e.g. of camera)	la marca
police station	la comisaría
thief	el ladrón

VERBS

to contain	contener
to describe	describir
to find	encontrar
to leave (behind)	dejar
to lend	prestar
to lose	perder
to run away	irse corriendo
to steal	robar

Te toca a ti

1 Say that you have lost something. Find out where the police station is.

2 Say that you have found something. Find out where the lost property office is.

3 Say the camera is quite large.

4 Say that you do not know the make.

5 Say that you bought it two years ago.

6 Say that it is five years old.

7 Tell the policeman that it is worth £100.

8 Say that the suitcase contained clothes, a watch and a gold ring.

9 Say that the purse contained twenty pounds.

10 Say that the wallet contained ten thousand pesetas.

11 Say that you did not see the thief.

¿Vd. ha perdido su esposa? Sí, ella está aquí . . .

12 Say that you lost it in front of the ticket-office.

13 Say that you left it in your room.

14 Say that the suitcase was in your father's car.

15 Say that you lost it two hours ago/yesterday/the day before yesterday.

16 Ask if the ring has been found.

17 Say that you are a British tourist.

18 Say that the handbag is your sister's.

19 Say that the camera is yours.

20 Ask if you must pay.

21 Ask what you must do now.

22 Say that you will return tomorrow.

23 Say that you will write.

24 Say that you will phone.

25 Say that your car has been stolen.

26 Say that a lot of things have been stolen from your car.

27 Say that you have lost your traveller's cheques/passport.

28 Ask him/her if he/she can lend you some money.

29 Say that you will lend him/her some money.

30 Say that the thief ran away.

31 Say it was a present from your aunt.

Las contestaciones están en la página 83

At the tourist information office

PLACES TO GO

amusements	**las diversiones**
circus	**el circo**
concert	**el concierto**
disco	**la discoteca**
museum	**el museo**
place of interest	**el sitio de interés**
show	**el espectáculo**
theatre	**el teatro**
trip	**la excursión**
zoo	**el jardín zoológico**

INFORMATION

brochure or leaflet	**el folleto**
information	**la información**

map of the area	**el mapa de la región**
map of the city	**el plano de la ciudad**
timetable	**el horario**

OTHER WORDS

information office	**la oficina de información**
ticket	**la entrada**
tourist office	**la oficina de turismo**

VERBS

to book	**reservar**
to go for walks	**ir de paseo**
to hire	**alquilar**
to interest	**interesar**
to visit	**visitar**

Te toca a ti

1 Say you are a British tourist.

2 Ask if he/she can give you information on the area.

3 Find out if he/she has any brochures.

4 Ask for a map of the city.

5 Ask for a map of the area.

6 Ask for a bus timetable.

7 Ask for a list of hotels and campsites.

8 Find out what the places of interest are.

9 Ask for information about the castle.

10 Say you would like information about the museum.

11 Find out if there are any trips.

12 Ask what there is to do in the evenings.

13 Find out if there are any shows/amusements.

14 Find out what time the museum opens/closes.

15 Say you like sports. Find out if there are any facilities.

16 Ask if you can hire skis/a bicycle.

17 Ask if you can buy tickets here.

¿Vd. quiere visitar el castillo? Muy bien, señorita.

18 Find out if there is a circus/theatre/concert in the area.

19 Say you are interested in castles.

Las contestaciones están en la página 84

Asking the way

VOCABULARIO ESENCIAL

DIRECTIONS		at the end of	al final de
straight on	**todo recto**	before	**antes de**
to (on) the left	**a la izquierda**	behind	**detrás de**
to (on) the right	**a la derecha**	beside	**al lado de**
		five kilometres away	**a cinco kilómetros**
HOW TO GET THERE		five minutes away	**a cinco minutos**
by bus	**en autobús**	opposite	**enfrente de**
by taxi	**en taxi**		
by train	**en tren**	**OTHER WORDS**	
by underground	**en metro**	area	**la región**
on foot	**a pie**	first	**primero**
		map (of town)	**el plano**
LANDMARKS		motorway	**la autopista**
bridge	**el puente**	road-map	**el mapa de carreteras**
bus stop	**la parada de autobuses**	second	**segundo**
city centre	**el centro de la ciudad**	**VERBS**	
corner	**la esquina**	to carry on	**continuar**
crossroads	**el cruce**	to cross	**cruzar**
roundabout	**la glorieta**	to follow	**seguir**
traffic-lights	**los semáforos**	to get lost	**perderse**
		to go down	**bajar**
POSITION		to go up	**subir**
after	**después de**		

Te toca a ti

1 Say 'Excuse me' to a passer-by.

2 Say that you are lost.

3 Ask for directions to the city centre.

4 Ask if it is far.

5 Ask how far it is.

6 Tell him/her to turn right at the crossroads.

7 Tell him/her to turn left after the bank.

8 Tell him/her to cross the bridge and go straight on.

9 Tell him/her to go up the road to the supermarket.

10 Tell him/her to go down the road as far as the traffic lights.

11 Say it is opposite the cinema.

12 Tell him/her to follow the road as far as the roundabout.

13 Say the bus-stop is on the left.

14 Tell him/her to take the first road on the right.

15 Tell him/her to take the second road after the bus stop.

16 Tell him/her to go straight on as far as the corner of the street.

17 Find out if he/she has a road-map/map of the town.

18 Tell him/her to take the motorway.

19 Say that you do not know the area.

20 Tell him/her that it is five kilometres away.

21 Say it is five minutes' walk away.

22 Tell him/her to take a taxi/tube/bus.

23 Tell him/her that it is behind the baker's.

24 Find out what number bus you must take.

25 Say that you will go with him/her.

26 Tell him/her to go down the corridor and take the lift to the first floor.

27 Say you do not understand.

28 Ask him/her to repeat that.

29 Ask where you can find a taxi.

Las contestaciones están en la página 85

¿Vd. va a Marte? Siga todo recto hasta la luna. Tuerza a la izquierda, siga por dos años y ¡ya está!

At the cinema

VOCABULARIO ESENCIAL

TYPES OF FILM

adventure film	la película de aventuras
comedy film	la película de risa
detective film	la película policíaca
horror film	la película de terror
romantic film	la película romántica
science-fiction film	la película de ciencia-ficción
spy film	la película de espionaje
war film	la película de guerra
western	la película del oeste

DETAILS OF FILM

original version	la versión original
performance	la sesión
star	la estrella
subtitles	los subtítulos

GETTING TO YOUR SEAT

tip	la propina
usherette	el acomodador / la acomodadora

OTHER WORDS

circle	el anfiteatro
interval	el descanso
reduction (in price)	la rebaja
stalls	la butaca
to book a ticket	reservar una entrada
to show (a film)	poner

Te toca a ti

1 Ask your friend what film is showing at the cinema.

2 Find out if the film has subtitles.

3 Find out if the film is in Spanish.

4 Say you would like to book two seats.

5 Ask your friend if he/she would like to go to the cinema this evening.

6 Ask your friend if you must give a tip to the usherette.

7 Find out what time the film starts.

8 Find out what time the film finishes.

9 Find out if there is an interval.

10 Ask how much a seat in the circle costs.

11 Say you would like a seat in the stalls.

12 Say that you liked the film.

13 Say that you did not like the film.

14 Find out if there is a reduction for groups.

15 Say that you prefer detective films.

16 Suggest that you meet in front of the cinema.

17 Ask what sort of film it is.

18 When your friend says it was a bad film, say that you do not agree.

19 Ask your friend if he/she liked the film.

20 When your friend says the film was good, say you agree.

21 Say you like adventure films/westerns/war films/spy films.

22 Say you do not like comedy films/horror films/romantic films/science fiction films.

23 Ask who the star of the film is.

Las contestaciones están en la página 86

At the hotel

VOCABULARIO ESENCIAL

TYPES OF ROOM

double room	la habitación doble
room with double bed	la habitación con cama doble
room with single bed	la habitación con cama individual
room with two single beds	la habitación con dos camas individuales
single room	la habitación individual

PLACES

bathroom	el cuarto de baño
car-park	el aparcamiento
corridor	el pasillo
floor (i.e. storey)	el piso
ground floor	la planta baja
lift	el ascensor
shower	la ducha
toilets	los servicios

CHECKING IN AND OUT

bed	la cama
bill	la cuenta
cheque	el cheque
credit card	la tarjeta de crédito
free (i.e. not occupied)	libre
full	lleno

full board and lodging	la pensión completa
half board	la media pensión
included	incluido
luggage	el equipaje
number	el número
suitcase	la maleta

ITEMS YOU MIGHT NEED

blanket	la manta
coat-hanger	la percha
key	la llave
pillow	la almohada
soap	el jabón
toilet-paper	el papel higiénico
towel	la toalla

COMPLAINTS

blocked	atrancado
noise	el ruido
tap	el grifo
too much	demasiado

VERBS

to book	reservar
to drip	gotear
to fill in a form	llenar una ficha
to park	aparcar
to work (i.e. to function	funcionar

Te toca a ti

1 Say you would like to book a room.

2 Say that you have booked a room.

3 Say that you would like a single room.

4 Say that you would like a double room.

5 Say that you would like a room with a single bed.

6 Say that you would like a room with a double bed.

7 Say that you would like a room with twin beds.

8 Ask if they have a room with a shower or a bathroom.

9 Say that you will stay for four nights.

10 Say that you would like to leave tomorrow morning.

11 Tell the receptionist that you would like to leave early.

12 Say that you want a room on the ground floor.

13 Ask what floor your room is on.

14 Find out the number of your room.

15 Find out if they serve meals.

16 Ask what time breakfast is served.

17 Ask if breakfast is included.

18 Ask if they have a room free.

19 Say you are English/Irish/Scottish/Welsh.

20 Find out if you have to fill in a form.

21 Ask for your key.

22 Ask for your bill.

23 Say the bill is not correct.

24 Tell the receptionist that you would like to pay by cheque or credit card.

25 Find out if there is a cinema nearby.

26 Ask for directions to the dining-room.

27 Say that there is no soap in your room.

28 Say that you would like an extra pillow.

29 Say that you are not happy with your room. Ask them to phone another hotel.

30 Say you would like to complain.

31 Say that there is no towel in your room.

32 Say that you have lost your key.

33 Find out if they have anything cheaper.

34 Ask if you can take up your luggage now.

35 Find out if there is a car-park nearby.

36 Say your room doesn't look onto the beach.

37 Say you will take these rooms.

38 Tell the receptionist that you have reserved a room by telephone.

39 Tell the receptionist that the lift doesn't work.

40 Say you would like more coat-hangers.

41 Say that the tap is leaking.

42 Say that the light is not working.

43 Say that the wash-basin is blocked.

44 Say that your room is too noisy.

45 Tell the receptionist that you want a different room.

46 Ask the receptionist for another blanket.

Las contestaciones están en la página 87

Visiting and receiving an exchange partner

VOCABULARIO ESENCIAL

ON ARRIVAL

clothes	**la ropa**
pleased to meet you	**encantado**
present (i.e. gift)	**el regalo**
suitcase	**la maleta**
tired	**cansado**
tiring	**cansador**
Welcome!	**¡Bienvenido!**

IN THE BATHROOM

bath	**el baño**
shower	**la ducha**
soap	**el jabón**
toothpaste	**la pasta de dientes**
towel	**la toalla**

DESCRIBING YOURSELF OVER THE PHONE

curly (hair)	**rizado**
fat	**gordo**
glasses	**las gafas**
long (hair)	**largo**
quite	**bastante**
short (hair)	**corto**
small (height)	**bajo**
straight (hair)	**liso**
tall	**alto**
thin	**delgado**

OTHER WORDS

downstairs	**abajo**
party	**la fiesta**
upstairs	**arriba**

VERBS

to clear the table	**quitar la mesa**
to do the washing-up	**lavar los platos**
to get to know	**conocer**
to go to bed	**acostarse**
to help	**ayudar**
to hurt oneself	**hacerse daño**
to introduce	**presentar**
to lay the table	**poner la mesa**
to lend	**prestar**
to rest	**descansar**
to share	**compartir**
to show	**mostrar**

Te toca a ti

1 Say that you are pleased to meet him/her.

2 Say that he/she is welcome.

3 Introduce him/her to your brother.

4 Say that it is a present from your parents.

5 Say that you have a brother and two sisters.

6 Find out where your room/the bathroom is.

7 Say you will show him/her to his/her room.

8 Tell him/her that the bathroom is upstairs, on the left.

9 Say that you would like to phone your parents.

10 Ask if he/she would like to phone his/her parents.

11 Find out what time breakfast is.

12 Tell your partner that breakfast is at eight o'clock.

13 Say you are tired and that you would like to go to bed.

14 Ask if he/she is tired.

15 Find out if he/she wants to go to bed.

16 Say that the journey was very tiring.

17 Say that you don't like Spanish food.

18 Ask if he/she likes English food.

19 Say that you do not like garlic.

20 Ask if he/she likes omlettes.

21 Find out what time you leave tomorrow.

22 Ask where you can put your clothes.

23 Ask where you can put your suitcase.

24 Ask where you can meet.

25 Say you would like to meet his/her friends.

26 Ask if he/she would like to meet your friends.

27 Ask if he/she wants to go to the swimming-pool.

28 Find out what he/she wants to do.

29 Say you would like to go out.

30 Say that you would like to go to the beach.

31 Suggest that you meet outside the station.

32 You are phoning your exchange partner. Say that you are tall/small.

33 Say that you wear glasses.

¡No quiero compartir una habitación!

34 Say that your hair is short/long.

35 Say that your hair is curly/straight.

36 Say that your hair is brown/black/fair.

37 Say that you will be wearing a green coat and jeans.

38 Say that you feel ill.

39 Say that you have hurt yourself.

40 Ask what he/she will be wearing.

41 Ask if he/she is ill.

42 Find out if he/she has hurt himself/herself.

43 Find out where you can wash your dirty clothes.

44 Ask if he/she has any dirty clothes.

45 Ask if you can watch the television.

46 Ask him/her if he/she wants to watch the television.

47 Say you would like to help his/her mother.

48 Say you will lay/clear the table.

49 Offer to wash the dishes.

50 Say that you would like to go to the party.

51 Ask if he/she wants to go to the party.

52 Find out how you will get back from the city centre.

53 Say that you can come back by bus.

54 Say that you do not want to share a room.

55 Ask if he/she has soap/a towel/toothpaste.

56 Say that you need soap/a towel/toothpaste.

57 Ask if he/she would like a shower/a bath.

58 Say that you would like to have a bath/shower.

59 Say that you are hungry/thirsty/hot/cold.

60 Say you would like to rest.

61 Ask if he/she can lend you some money.

Las contestaciones están en la página 90

Las contestaciones

Public transport

1 Quiero un billete de ida de segunda clase a Madrid.

2 Quiero un billete de primera clase de ida y vuelta a Valencia.

3 Quiero dos billetes.

4 ¿Hay un autocar/un tren a Barcelona?

5 ¿A qué hora llega/sale?

6 ¿Cúando salen los trenes para Madrid?

7 Quiero reservar un billete.

8 He reservado un billete.

9 ¿Dónde está la estación/la estación de autobuses/la estación del metro?

10 ¿Cuánto tiempo dura el viaje?

11 ¿Cuándo sale el próximo vuelo?

12 ¿Dónde está el despacho de billetes?

13 ¿Dónde está la oficina de información?

14 ¿Dónde está la consigna/la oficina de objetos perdidos?

15 ¿De dónde sale el tren para Madrid?

16 ¿De qué andén sale el tren para Valencia?

17 ¿Dónde está la parada de taxis/la parada de autobuses?

18 ¿Hay un asiento libre en el vagón?

19 El asiento está ocupado.

20 ¿A qué hora sale/llega el avión?

21 Quiero tomar un taxi.

22 ¿Dónde puedo encontrar un taxi?

23 ¿El tren es directo?

24 ¿Hay que hacer transbordo?

25 ¿Dónde hay que hacer transbordo?

26 Quiero un hotel barato.

27 ¿Dónde está la cafetería?

28 ¿Cuándo sale el próximo/primer/último autocar?

29 Quiero un departamento de no fumadores.

30 ¿Dónde puedo poner mi equipaje?

31 ¿Es éste el andén del tren para Santander?

32 ¿Dónde tengo que bajar?

33 ¿Hay un coche-comedor/un coche-cama?

34 ¿Hay una rebaja/un suplemento?

35 ¿Dónde están los servicios?

36 ¿Dónde está la sala de espera?

37 ¿Puedo dejar mi equipaje aquí?

38 ¿El vuelo va a llegar tarde?

39 ¿El tren llegó temprano?

40 He perdido mi billete.

41 Quiero un plano del metro, por favor.

42 Llegaré a las diez de la tarde.

43 Me marcho a las dos de la madrugada.

44 ¿Tienes algo que declarar?

45 Acabo de llegar.

46 Tomaré el autocar de las diez.

47 Intenté llamar desde la estación.

48 Llamaré desde el aeropuerto.

49 ¿Dónde puedo encontrar un mozo?

50 ¿Quiere Vd. ayudarme con mi equipaje?

51 He perdido el autocar.

52 ¿El autobús va al centro de la ciudad?

At the garage/filling station

1 Quiero veinte litros de súper.

2 Quiero diez litros de gasolina sin plomo.

3 Lleno, por favor.

4 ¿Quiere Vd. comprobar el aceite?

5 ¿Quiere Vd. comprobar los neumáticos?

6 ¿Quiere Vd. comprobar el agua?

7 ¿Dónde están los servicios?

8 ¿Vende Vd. mapas de carreteras?

9 ¿Es ésta la carretera para Madrid?

10 ¿Por dónde se va a Málaga?

11 ¿Es una carretera nacional o una autopista?

12 ¿Dónde puedo aparcar?

13 Mi coche se ha averiado.

14 Lo he dejado a dos kilómetros de aquí.

15 ¿Puede Vd. ayudar?

16 ¿Puede Vd. reparar mi coche?

17 ¿Hay un mecánico?

18 Los frenos no funcionan.

19 Tengo un pinchazo.

20 Un faro no funciona.

21 El parabrisas está roto.

22 Necesito una batería nueva.

23 ¿Cuánto le debo?

24 ¿Puedo telefonear desde aquí?

25 ¿A qué distancia está Madrid?

26 ¿Dónde está el hotel más cercano?

27 ¿Vende Vd. caramelos?

28 ¿Quiere Vd. limpiar el parabrisas?

29 Me he quedado sin gasolina.

30 He tenido un accidente.

31 ¿Cuánto tiempo tendré que esperar?

32 ¿Cuánto costará?

At the customs

1 Soy inglés (inglesa)/irlandés (irlandesa)/escocés (escocesa)/
galés (galesa).

2 No tengo nada que declarar.

3 Quiero declarar una máquina fotográfica.

4 Tengo dos maletas y un bolso.

5 Esta maleta es mía.

6 Hay ropa y regalos en mi maleta.

7 Compré el reloj en Suiza hace dos semanas.

8 El perfume costó cuatro mil pesetas.

9 ¿Quiere Vd. ver mi pasaporte?

10 Estaré en España dos semanas.

11 Estoy aquí de vacaciones.

At the campsite

1 Quiero reservar un sitio.

2 ¿Puedo acampar aquí?

3 ¿Hay sitio para una tienda?

4 Tengo una tienda/una caravana.

5 ¿Cuánto es para una tienda, dos adultos, cuatro niños y un coche?

6 Quiero quedarme dos noches.

7 Estoy solo(a).

8 Llegaré pasado mañana.

9 Me voy el sábado.

10 ¿Dónde puedo montar mi tienda?

11 Quiero un sitio en la sombra.

12 Soy inglés (inglesa)/irlandés (irlandesa)/escocés (escocesa)/ galés (galesa).

13 ¿Quiere Vd. ver mi pasaporte?

14 ¿Cuándo tengo que pagar?

15 Quiero pagar ahora.

16 ¿Cómo se va al camping?

17 ¿Hay duchas con agua caliente?

18 Quiero un sitio cerca de los servicios.

19 ¿Dónde hay agua potable?

20 ¿Dónde puedo lavar ropa/los platos?

21 ¿Cuál es el reglamento?

22 Mi tienda está demasiado cerca de los cubos de basura.

23 ¿Quiere Vd. prestarme un abrelatas/un sacacorchos/cerillas?

24 ¿Puedo montar mi tienda allí?

25 ¿Dónde está la toma de corriente más cercana?

26 ¿Cuánto es por persona?

27 Es demasiado caro.

28 ¿Hay una lavadora en el camping?

29 ¿Vds. sirven comidas calientes?

30 ¿Hay una tienda en el camping?

31 ¿Puedo hacer fuego?

32 Me gusta mucho el camping.

33 ¿El camping tiene muchas instalaciones?

34 Necesito gas butano.

35 Necesito pilas.

36 ¿El camping está bien iluminado por la noche?

37 ¿El camping está cerrado por la noche?

38 ¿Hay que pagar un suplemento?

At the youth hostel

1 He reservado una cama.

2 No he reservado una cama.

3 ¿Hay camas?

4 Me marcho mañana/pasado mañana.

5 Me quedo tres noches.

6 Somos dos chicos y dos chicas.

7 Soy inglés (inglesa)/irlandés (irlandesa)/escocés (escocesa)/galés (galesa).

8 ¿Cuánto es por persona?

9 ¿Hay tiendas cerca de aquí?

10 ¿Hay duchas/una cocina en el albergue juvenil?

11 ¿Dónde están los servicios/los cubos de basura?

12 Quiero pagar ahora/más tarde/mañana/al marcharme.

13 ¿A qué hora es el desayuno/el almuerzo/la cena?

14 ¿A qué hora cierra el albergue?

15 ¿A qué hora abre la oficina por la mañana?

16 ¿Cuál es el reglamento?

17 Tengo un saco de dormir.

18 Quiero alquilar un saco de dormir/sábanas/mantas.

19 ¿Dónde está el dormitorio de las chicas/de los chicos?

20 ¿Se permite alcohol?

21 ¿A qué hora tengo que salir del albergue?

22 ¿Hay que rellenar una ficha?

23 ¿Hay agua caliente?

24 ¿Qué hay que hacer antes de marcharse?

25 ¿Dónde puedo dejar los objetos de valor?

26 Tengo una queja.

27 ¿Quiere Vd. ver mi pasaporte?

28 ¿El albergue está lleno?

29 ¿El albergue está abierto todo el año?

30 ¿Puedo cocinar en el albergue?

31 ¿Se sirven comidas?

32 ¿Dónde está el comedor?

33 ¿Dónde puedo dejar mi bicicleta?

34 Lo siento. No quiero una cama arriba. Quiero una cama en la planta baja.

At the doctor's/at the scene of an accident

1 ¿Puede ayudarme?

2 ¿Quiere Vd. llamar a un médico?

3 ¿Quiere Vd. llamar una ambulancia?

4 Necesito ver a un dentista.

5 Quiero ver al médico.

6 He tenido un accidente.

7 Me duele una muela.

8 Me duele la garganta.

9 Me duele la cabeza.

10 Me duele el estómago.

11 Tengo el brazo roto/la pierna rota.

12 Tiene el brazo roto/la pierna rota.

13 Estoy constipado(a).

14 Me he quemado.

15 Me he quemado el brazo.

16 Tiene una insolación/una quemadura del sol.

17 Tengo la gripe.

18 Me he cortado.

19 Me he cortado en la pierna.

20 Me he caído.

21 He tenido un accidente de coche.

22 Tengo fiebre.

23 Estoy mareado(a).

24 Algo me ha picado.

25 Toso mucho.

26 He vomitado tres veces.

27 Mi amigo está herido.

28 ¿Tengo que venir otra vez para ver al médico?

29 ¿Tengo que guardar cama?

30 ¿Necesito una receta?

31 ¿Dónde está la farmacia?

32 Un recibo, por favor.

33 ¿Cuánto tiempo tengo que tomar las pastillas?

34 Quiero comprar algodón hidrófilo, una venda, esparadrapo y un antiséptico.

35 Mi hermana se siente enferma.

36 Quiero aspirinas, por favor.

37 Dos horas/desde ayer.

38 ¿Cúantas veces al día tengo que tomar las pastillas?

39 Me siento enfermo(a)/mejor.

40 ¿Tiene algo para el dolor de garganta?

41 No estoy tomando medicinas.

42 Tengo un seguro.

43 ¿Quiere Vd. llamar a la policía/a los bomberos?

44 El accidente fue grave.

45 No fue culpa mía. Fue la culpa del otro conductor.

46 ¿Tiene una pomada para quemaduras del sol?

47 Mi padre frenó pero hubo una colisión.

48 Hubo un incendio en el motor.

49 El permiso de conducir de mi padre está en el hotel.

50 Un ciclista atropelló a un viejo que cruzaba la calle.

51 Me duele.

Shopping for food and drink

1 Quiero una barra de pan, por favor.

2 ¿Cuánto es?

3 Quiero comprar pasteles.

4 Quinientos gramos de jamón, por favor.

5 Quiero carne de vaca.

6 Doscientos cincuenta gramos de chorizo.

7 ¿Hay una tienda de comestibles abierta por aquí?

8 Quiero comprar cigarrillos para mi padre.

9 Quiero doscientos gramos de ciruelas/plátanos/naranjas/
melocotones/peras/manzanas/fresas/albaricoques/uvas.

10 Una piña/un melón, por favor.

11 ¿Dónde puedo comprar legumbres?

12 Judías verdes/cebollas/guisantes/patatas/champiñones/
zanahorias/una coliflor.

13 Una lechuga, por favor.

14 ¿Hay una carnicería por aquí?

15 Un pollo/un conejo/quinientos gramos de carne de vaca, por favor.

16 ¿La carne de aquella carnicería es buena?

17 ¿Dónde puedo comprar mariscos?

18 ¿Tiene Vd. vino francés?

19 Dos litros de vino tinto y un litro de vino blanco, por favor.

20 Cinco litros de cerveza, por favor.

21 Café, por favor.

22 Una botella de agua mineral, por favor.

23 Quiero zumo de fruta, por favor.

24 Un litro de leche, por favor.

25 Un paquete de té, por favor.

26 Una docena de huevos, por favor.

27 ¿Dónde puedo comprar sal/pimienta?

28 Doscientos gramos de queso, por favor.

29 Estoy comprando comida para una merienda.

30 Doscientos gramos de mantequilla, por favor.

31 ¿Vende Vd. caramelos/chocolate?

32 Un paquete de azúcar, por favor.

33 No me gusta. No voy a comprar.

34 Es demasiado caro.

35 Vd. me ha dado demasiado/muy poco.

36 Me lo llevo.

37 Nada más, gracias.

38 ¿Cuánto le debo?

39 ¿Tiene Vd. cambio para el teléfono?

40 Compré este queso aquí. No es bueno. ¿Quiere Vd. devolverme mi dinero?

41 Tengo solamente un billete de mil pesetas.

42 ¿Puedo escoger la fruta que quiero?

43 Un poco más grande, por favor.

44 ¿Tiene Vd. algo más barato?

45 ¿Dónde está la caja?

46 ¿Tiene Vd. una caja/una bolsa de plástico?

47 ¿Puedo pagar con cheque o con tarjeta de crédito?

48 ¿Vds. están abiertos el domingo?

49 ¿A qué hora abre/cierra?

Shopping for clothes and toiletries

1 ¿Cuál es la talla?

2 ¿Cuál es el número de los zapatos?

3 ¿La camisa es de algodón/nilón?

4 ¿El jersey es de lana?

5 Quiero comprar zapatillas.

6 ¿Los guantes son de cuero?

7 Me gusta esta chaqueta.

8 ¿Dónde están los probadores?

9 Quiero probarme este pantalón.

10 ¿Tiene la misma falda en azul?

11 El vestido es demasiado largo/corto/estrecho/ancho/
grande/pequeño.

12 ¿Quiere Vd. envolver esta bufanda en papel de regalo?

13 ¿En qué piso está la sección de caballeros?

14 ¿Dónde está la caja?

15 ¿Dónde está el ascensor/la salida?

16 ¿A qué hora abren/cierran?

17 ¿Puedo escuchar este disco?

18 ¿Tiene Vd. una bolsa de plástico?

19 ¿Puedo cambiar el abrigo?

20 No es mi talla.

21 ¿Hay otra tienda cerca de aquí?

22 Vd. se ha equivocado.

23 ¿Qué vas a comprar?

24 ¿Esta camiseta me va?

25 ¿Dónde puedo comprar jabón/champú/un peine/un cepillo de
dientes/pasta de dientes?

26 Quiero ir de escaparates.

27 Es demasiado caro.

28 Es muy barato.

29 ¿Tiene mi talla?

30 ¿Tiene Vd. algo más barato?

31 ¿Dónde pago?

At the cleaner's/launderette

1 ¿Puede Vd. limpiar/limpiar en seco este pantalón?

2 ¿Puede Vd. reparar esta blusa?

3 ¿Cuánto tiempo hace falta?

4 Quiero lavar esta ropa.

5 ¿Tiene Vd. cambio para la lavadora?

6 ¿Qué monedas necesito para la lavadora?

7 ¿Dónde puedo comprar jabón en polvo?

At the café/restaurant

1 Señor/señora/señorita. El menú, por favor.

2 Quiero dejar una propina.

3 Quiero reservar una mesa.

4 He reservado una mesa.

5 Una taza/un platillo/un cuchillo/un tenedor/una cuchara/un vaso, por favor.

6 El mantel está sucio.

7 Quiero pedir ahora.

8 ¿Quiere Vd. quitar su bandeja?

9 La cuenta, por favor.

10 ¡Salud! ¡Qué aproveche!

11 ¿Quiere Vd. escoger el vino?

12 ¿Dónde está el teléfono/¿Dónde están los servicios?

13 ¿El servicio está incluido?

14 Tengo hambre/sed.

15 Quiero el bistec poco hecho/medio hecho/bien hecho.

16 La comida es deliciosa.

17 ¿Qué vas a tomar de postre?

18 Me siento enfermo(a).

19 Quiero el menú turístico.

20 Quiero el menú del día.

21 Chuleta de cerdo con cebollas, guisantes y patatas.

22 ¿Vd. sirve desayuno?

23 Quiero café solo/con leche.

24 Sopa, conejo y arroz/patatas.

25 Quiero un bocadillo de queso/de chorizo/de jamón.

26 Quiero ostras/mejillones.

27 Quiero trucha/sardinas.

28 Quiero pepino en la ensalada.

29 Quiero ciruelas/un plátano/un melón/una naranja/un melocotón/
una pera/una manzana/fresas/albaricoques/piña/uvas.

30 Quiero pollo, judías verdes, champiñones y zanahorias.

31 No me gusta el ajo.

32 La coliflor no es buena.

33 ¿Hay cordero?

34 ¿Qué hay de beber?

35 Un litro de vino blanco/tinto.

36 Medio litro de cerveza.

37 Quiero zumo de fruta/agua mineral/leche/té.

38 Quiero un huevo pasado por agua/frito/escalfado/revuelto.

39 ¿Hay sal/pimienta/vinagre/mostaza?

40 Una ración de jamón.

41 ¿Quiere Vd. limpiar la mesa?

42 Quiero estar fuera, en el sol/en la sombra.

43 Una mesa para dos cerca de la ventana.

44 Vd. se ha equivocado.

45 No entiendo el menú. ¿Qué es este plato?

46 ¿Quiere Vd. cerrar/abrir la ventana?

47 Más, por favor.

48 Un cenicero, por favor.

49 Vd. ha olvidado el helado de vainilla.

50 ¿Tiene cambio para el teléfono?

51 La comida está fría.

52 Mi tenedor está sucio.

53 Quiero algo fresco/caliente para beber.

54 Tengo calor/tengo frío.

55 Tomamos solamente una limonada y un zumo de naranja.

56 ¿Quiere Vd. mirar la cuenta otra vez?

57 Tengo prisa. ¿Cuánto tiempo falta?

58 Somos cuatro.

59 El plato no es carne, sino pescado.

60 Vds. aceptan tarjetas de crédito?

61 No pedí vino.

62 ¿Hay una selección de legumbres?

63 Huele bien.

64 ¿Has decidido?

65 Es demasiado caro.

66 ¿Qué vino quieres?

At the post office

1 ¿Por dónde se va a la oficina de Correos?

2 ¿Hay un buzón en la oficina de Correos?

3 ¿Cuánto cuesta mandar una carta/una postal a Inglaterra?

4 Quiero mandar una carta a Gran Bretaña.

5 Quiero mandar un paquete.

6 ¿Hay un paquete aquí para mí?

7 Quiero dos sellos de cuarenta pesetas.

8 ¿A qué hora abre/cierra?

9 ¿Hay una carta para mí en la lista de correos?

10 ¿Hay una cabina telefónica allí?

11 Necesito monedas para una llamada al Reino Unido.

12 Quiero mandar un telegrama.

13 ¿Cuánto cuesta mandar un telegrama?

14 ¿En cuántos días llegará una carta al Reino Unido?

15 ¿Hay un buzón especial para cartas al extranjero?

16 ¿Dónde hay un buzón?

17 Quiero telefonear a Inglaterra.

18 Quiero comprar un giro postal.

19 ¿Qué ventanilla es?

20 Quiero mandar la carta por avión.

21 ¿Hay que rellenar una ficha?

22 ¿La oficina de Correos está abierta el sábado?

23 ¿Hay un servicio más rápido?

24 ¿Cuándo es la próxima recogida?

On the telephone

1 ¿Dónde está el teléfono más cercano?

2 La guía telefónica, por favor.

3 ¿Puedo hablar con Juan?

4 No entiendo el tono de marcar.

5 El número de la oficina de turismo, por favor.

6 Quiero hablar con la operadora.

7 Quiero hacer una llamada a cobro revertido.

8 Hola. Soy Melanie.

9 ¿Quiere Vd. dejar un recado?

10 No entiendo. ¿Quiere Vd. hablar más despacio?

11 No cuelgue.

12 Me he equivocado de número.

At the bank/exchange office

1 ¿Dónde tengo que hacer cola?

2 Quiero cambiar unas libras en pesetas.

3 Quiero cambiar cheques de viaje en pesetas.

4 ¿Qué ventanilla, por favor?

5 ¿Me toca a mí?

6 ¿A cómo está el cambio?

7 ¿Quiere Vd. ver mi pasaporte?

8 He olvidado mi pasaporte.

9 Voy a buscar mi pasaporte.

10 ¿Dónde tengo que firmar?

11 ¿Cuánto vale la libra?

12 ¿Tengo que ir a la ventanilla de pagos?

13 Tengo una tarjeta de crédito.

14 Tengo una tarjeta bancaria.

15 ¿Tengo que pagar una comisión?

16 ¿La comisión es el diez por ciento?

17 Quiero billetes de cinco mil pesetas.

18 Quiero monedas de cien pesetas.

19 Me han robado todo mi dinero.

20 ¿Quiere Vd. llamar a mi banco en Inglaterra?

At the police station/ lost-property office

1 He perdido algo. ¿Dónde está la comisaría?

2 He encontrado algo. ¿Dónde está la oficina de objetos perdidos?

3 La máquina fotográfica es bastante grande.

4 No sé la marca.

5 Lo (la) compré hace dos años.

6 Tiene cinco años.

7 Vale cien libras.

8 La maleta contenía ropa, un reloj y un anillo de oro.

9 El monedero contenía veinte libras.

10 La cartera contenía diez mil pesetas.

11 No vi al ladrón.

12 Lo (la) perdí delante del despacho de billetes.

13 Lo (la) dejé en mi habitación.

14 La maleta estaba en el coche de mi padre.

15 Lo (la) perdí hace dos horas/ayer/anteayer.

16 ¿Alguien ha encontrado el anillo?

17 Soy turista británico(a).

18 El bolso de mano es de mi hermana.

19 La máquina fotográfica es mía.

20 ¿Tengo que pagar?

21 ¿Qué tengo que hacer ahora?

22 Volveré mañana.

23 Le escribiré.

24 Telefonearé.

25 Me han robado mi coche.

26 Me han robado muchas cosas de mi coche.

27 He perdido mis cheques de viaje/mi pasaporte.

28 ¿Puede Vd. prestarme dinero?

29 Yo le prestaré dinero.

30 El ladrón se fue corriendo.

31 Fue un regalo de mi tía.

At the tourist information office

1 Soy turista británico(a).

2 ¿Puede Vd. darme información sobre la región?

3 ¿Tiene Vd. folletos?

4 Quiero un plano de la ciudad.

5 Quiero un mapa de la región.

6 Quiero un horario de los autobuses.

7 Quiero una lista de los hoteles y de los campings.

8 ¿Cuáles son los sitios de interés?

9 Quiero información sobre el castillo.

10 Quiero información sobre el museo.

11 ¿Hay excursiones?

12 ¿Qué se puede hacer por la tarde?

13 ¿Hay espectáculos/diversiones?

14 ¿A qué hora abre/cierra el museo?

15 Me gustan los deportes. ¿Hay facilidades?

16 ¿Puedo alquilar esquís/una bicicleta?

17 ¿Puedo comprar entradas aquí?

18 ¿Hay un circo/teatro/concierto en la región?

19 Me interesan los castillos.

Asking the way

1 Perdone, señor/señora/señorita.

2 Estoy perdido(a).

3 ¿Dónde está el centro de la ciudad?

4 ¿Está lejos?

5 ¿A qué distancia está?

6 Hay que ir a la derecha en el cruce.

7 Hay que ir a la izquierda después del banco.

8 Hay que cruzar el puente y continuar todo recto.

9 Hay que subir la calle hasta el supermercado.

10 Hay que bajar la calle hasta los semáforos.

11 Está enfrente del cine.

12 Hay que seguir la carretera hasta la glorieta.

13 La parada de autobuses está a la izquierda.

14 Tome la primera calle a la derecha.

15 Tome la segunda calle depués de la parada de autobuses.

16 Hay que ir todo recto hasta la esquina.

17 ¿Tiene Vd. un mapa de carreteras/plano de la ciudad?

18 Hay que tomar la autopista.

19 No conozco la región.

20 Está a cinco kilómetros de aquí.

21 Está a cinco minutos de aquí, andando.

22 Hay que tomar un taxi/el metro/un autobús.

23 Está detrás de la panadería.

24 ¿Cuál es el número del autobús?

25 Le acompañaré.

26 Hay que ir por el pasillo y tomar el ascensor al primer piso.

27 No entiendo.

28 ¿Quiere Vd. repetirlo?

29 ¿Dónde puedo encontrar un taxi?

At the cinema

1 ¿Qué ponen en el cine?

2 ¿La película tiene subtítulos?

3 ¿La película es en español?

4 Quiero reservar dos entradas.

5 ¿Quieres ir al cine esta tarde?

6 ¿Hay que dar una propina a la acomodadora?

7 ¿A qué hora empieza la película?

8 ¿A qué hora termina la película?

9 ¿Hay un descanso?

10 ¿Cuánto es una localidad de anfiteatro?

11 Quiero una localidad de butaca.

12 Me gustó la película.

13 No me gustó la película.

14 ¿Hay una rebaja para grupos?

15 Prefiero películas policíacas.

16 ¿Nos encontramos delante del cine?

17 ¿Qué tipo de película es?

18 No estoy de acuerdo.

19 ¿Te gustó la película?

20 Estoy de acuerdo.

21 Me gustan las películas de aventuras/del oeste/de guerra/de espionaje.

22 No me gustan las películas de risa/de terror/románticas/de ciencia-ficción.

23 ¿Quién es la estrella?

At the hotel

1 Quiero reservar una habitación.

2 He reservado una habitación.

3 Quiero una habitación individual.

4 Quiero una habitación doble.

5 Quiero una habitación con cama individual.

6 Quiero una habitación con cama doble.

7 Quiero una habitación con dos camas individuales.

8 ¿Tiene una habitación con ducha o cuarto de baño?

9 Me quedaré cuatro noches.

10 Quiero marcharme mañana por la mañana.

11 Quiero marcharme temprano.

12 Quiero una habitación en la planta baja.

13 ¿En qué piso está mi habitación?

14 ¿Cuál es el número de mi habitación?

15 ¿Vds. sirven comidas?

16 ¿A qué hora es el desayuno?

17 ¿El desayuno está incluido?

18 ¿Tiene una habitación libre?

19 Soy inglés (inglesa)/irlandés (irlandesa)/escocés (escocesa)/
galés (galesa).

20 ¿Hay que rellenar una ficha?

21 Mi llave, por favor.

22 La cuenta, por favor.

23 La cuenta no es correcta.

24 Quiero pagar con cheque o con tarjeta de crédito.

25 ¿Hay un cine cerca de aquí?

26 ¿Dónde está el comedor?

27 No hay jabón en mi habitación.

28 Quiero otra almohada.

29 No me gusta mi habitación. ¿Quiere Vd. llamar a otro hotel?

30 Tengo una queja.

31 No hay toalla en mi habitación.

32 He perdido mi llave.

33 ¿Tiene Vd. algo más barato?

34 ¿Puedo subir mi equipaje ahora?

35 ¿Hay un aparcamiento cerca de aquí?

36 Mi habitación no da a la playa.

37 Me quedo con estas habitaciones.

38 He reservado una habitación por teléfono.

39 El ascensor no funciona.

40 Quiero más perchas.

41 Hay un grifo que gotea.

42 La luz no funciona.

43 El lavabo está atrancado.

44 Hay demasiasdo ruido.

45 Quiero otra habitación.

46 Otra manta, por favor.

Visiting and receiving an exchange partner

1 Encantado(a).

2 Bienvenido(a).

3 Te presento a mi hermano.

4 Es un regalo de parte de mis padres.

5 Tengo un hermano y dos hermanas.

6 ¿Dónde está mi habitación/el cuarto de baño?

7 Te voy a mostrar tu habitación.

8 El cuarto de baño está arriba, a la izquierda.

9 Quiero llamar a mis padres.

10 ¿Quieres llamar a tus padres?

11 ¿A qué hora es el desayuno?

12 El desayuno es a las ocho.

13 Estoy cansado(a). Quiero ir a la cama.

14 ¿Estás cansado(a)?

15 ¿Quieres ir a la cama?

16 El viaje fue muy cansador.

17 No me gusta la comida española.

18 ¿Te gusta la comida inglesa?

19 No me gusta el ajo.

20 ¿Te gustan las tortillas?

21 ¿A qué hora te marchas mañana?

22 ¿Dónde puedo poner mi ropa?

23 ¿Dónde puedo poner mi maleta?

24 ¿Dónde nos encontraremos?

25 Quiero conocer a tus amigos.

26 ¿Quieres conocer a mis amigos?

27 ¿Quieres ir a la piscina?

28 ¿Qué quieres hacer?

29 Quiero salir.

30 Quiero ir a la playa.

31 ¿Nos encontraremos delante de la estación?

32 Soy alto(a) / bajo(a).

33 Llevo gafas.

34 Tengo el pelo corto / largo.

35 Tengo el pelo rizado / liso.

36 Tengo el pelo castaño / negro / rubio.

37 Llevaré un abrigo verde y vaqueros.

38 Me siento enfermo(a).

39 Me he hecho daño.

40 ¿Qué llevarás?

41 ¿Estás enfermo(a)?

42 ¿Te has hecho daño?

43 ¿Dónde puedo lavar mi ropa sucia?

44 ¿Tienes ropa sucia?

45 ¿Puedo ver la televisión?

46 ¿Quieres ver la televisión?

47 Quiero ayudar a tu madre.

48 Voy a poner / quitar la mesa.

49 Voy a lavar los platos.

50 Quiero ir a la fiesta.

51 ¿Quieres ir a la fiesta?

52 ¿Cómo voy a volver desde el centro de la ciudad?

53 Puedes volver en autobús.

54 No quiero compartir una habitación.

55 ¿Tienes jabón / una toalla / pasta de dientes?

56 Necesito jabón / una toalla / pasta de dientes.

57 ¿Quieres tomar una ducha / un baño?

58 Quiero tomar un baño / una ducha.

59 Tengo hambre / sed / calor / frío.

60 Quiero descansar.

61 ¿Puedes prestarme dinero?